Somethings Are Better Left Unsaid

Forgotten Poems

Christina Colvin

BookLeaf Publishing

India | USA | UK

Made with ❤ on the BookLeaf Publishing Platform
www.bookleafpub.in
www.bookleafpub.com

Dedication

this book is dedicated to every woman who has lived through the chapters of her own story and stands with her head held high to narrate it.

Preface

Acknowledgements

Thank You God.

1. Alice in the Wilderness

I found myself in an abysmal abyss
transliteration, death
I took an assessment of my health
I started walking
Then jogging
Then vehemently running
The destination, unknown
The cause of the issues, my own

Now Im in a strange place
A type of purgatory if you will
I'm miles away from self loathing and sabotage
But just outside the jurisdiction of self acceptance and
success
I hear echoes of debauchery in the distance
There are beams in my line of sight
Prophetic demonstrations of God interrupting my season
of night
But I'm still not close enough to feel the warmth of the
light

It's an unusual place indeed
I'm close enough to smell the flowers
But too far to plant my own seed

I cut myself just to see if it bleeds
Not cuz I'm suicidal
But Because this place feels like make believe
I feel like I'm in a scene
from Alice in Wonderland

I know that I'm awake but this is also not reality
To come this far and fail would be tragedy
I have no choice but to tap into my majesty
To manifest the quest of conquering spiritual death
And do it honestly

HONESTLY

Despite its elusiveness
I feel closer to my dreams than I've ever been
When I pick up the pen
I feel the sun.

2. Dandelions

Honestly
I got to be honest with me
I'm not satisfied with my choices
The self convicting voices are starting to get louder than
my weed
Every decision a seed
I'm paranoid
Cuz I know Im planting weeds
Then have the nerve to pray and ask for dandelions

3. Birds with Broken Wings

Birds with broken wings still fly
They still soar with ease
Their beauty lies in the effortlessness of their resiliency
pain doesn't stop purpose
An eagle is still an eagle
Injury isn't fatality
An eagle is still an eagle

4. Fragments

How can you experience such a great love and still not love yourself ?

Well, Everyday is a fight for peace and mental health

Peace I cry, PEACE

But the pieces are perplexing

Illustrating distressing

The piece cry's for peace but winds up with more pieces

Each telling its own story

To God be the glory

The architect of this puzzle

Only something super natural could hold these broken pieces together and make mosaic.

How can you experience such a great love and still not love yourself?

I only see the fragments. . . not the mosaic

5. Him

In hopeful expectation of your arrival

I patiently wait on you

It's like an ethereal pull on my spirit

I feel your heart beat

The things that trouble your mind find their way into my prayer time

I pray for you earnestly

I wonder if you know you're not alone

There's this hopeless devotion

My mind has traced your stature

My spirit has discerned your substance

I see you

even though I have yet to memorize the details of your
face.

6. Before the Vomit

Speak my peace , and let it go.
Ashamed of my emotions,
chained by my convulsions,
I cant even "look relaxed".
But if I'm afraid of my voice you'll move forward without
even looking back.

There you are, feet up, relaxed.
Satisfied, smoking your cigarette.
A thought emerges, Release that which keeps you in
bondage .
For you its A matter of physical detachment,
"let me Delete this thread, and oh yeah that attachment".
But its An out of body experience for me.
I gave you space in here
and you fucked me mentally.
Make it make sense to me.

I had faith in your hands and abilities.
I knew you would create a masterpiece for me.
So I brung you the finest thread,
but you took my offering and hung me instead.
I got mastered like a puppet

Given pieces of fabrication
I was fooled by the synthetic imitation.
You cloaked my ears with layered exaggeration.
I was blinded to the limitation.

Serpent.
No, better yet, Slithren suits you.
Lustfully illustrated deception.
Lisp lies lingured on your tongue.
Sometimes I would taste them when we kissed.

First there would be gooey eyes,
then butterflies
our tongues would tie
the butterflies intensify.
Amplified so much,
my stomach would feel flush.
Literally in knots,
spirit sick from digesting the plot.
in that moment I knew something wasn't right.
Little did I know the pain of the end
would mirror the sensation from this night.
The realization was blurred by temptation.
The play wasn't even flawless.
I'm still attracted to chaos and wanna be playas.
I mean don't get me wrong I know it's my fault.
I set myself up,

I knew I was fucked.
I was just hopeful I had stumbled across luck and you
was somebody I could trust.
Niggas be Lying tho,
I gotta just let this go.

But it's affecting me.
Got me Looking for defect in me
Stressing constantly
Like something's wrong with me

All that time spent
All that knowledge kicked
I deserved honesty
That's it.

You snatched the scab off this wound
Now im Bleeding out rapidly
Emotions reek havoc
You take a step back from me
I told you I wasn't healed
Your intentions, concealed
Now im open
But you just playing the field
you could have just kept it real
Give me the option to deal

That's my spill
Speak it and release it
Emotional vomit
Ejecting all my demons
I'm just looking for a reason
To feel something for more than a season

7. Beauty

You are beautiful beloved

The finest portrait painted by heaven's renowned craftsman

You are art

In all His glory

You are His heart

With a profound story

Like Noah's ark

Your body is a temple built from obedience

You are smart

Not by the worlds standards

But because you're humble enough to wait on Gods answers

I could talk about your beauty

But it wouldn't suffice

I could go on about your elegance

But we'd be here all night

Instead I'll say

You Radiate Gods Glory

And I'm in awe of you.

8. A Story of Rebirth

She was just a misunderstood girl from the eastside of Detroit, with dreams of being anything other than poor and ordinary. She loved God, fiction books, love stories, and adventure. She lived through theatre, expressed through poetry, and rejoiced in dance. But she sang like her heart was on fire. She was art.

A masterpiece delicately crafted with passion. One of one. But that meant alone. More often than not, she didn't fit in and she tried too hard. A confused swan surrounded by disgruntled ducks. The story of the ugly duckling echoed an uncomfortably familiar feeling. Dancing around in the hallowed spaces of her heart.

It was like being an antelope amongst hyenas. Poise, grace, and meekness didn't translate into majestic beast. No. It meant prey. Tender juicy meat. Nothing more than morsel to be devoured. Astounding speed only gets a doe but so far. Where can you really run when the hyena is in your home anyway.

To survive, she felt she had to change. She decided she would learn to shapeshift. The only way to keep the mustard-sized seed of hope alive was to hide it. She became what they wanted her to be. She became, whatever was required. She conformed to their expectations, but most importantly, she learned how to look and act like a predator, so she would never be prey.

The problem with that is, you get lost, and camouflaging quickly becomes people-pleasing. Before you know it, being what they want you to be, gets your foot caught in another bear trap, and eventually, you're prey again. But this time it's your facade that's under attack. Losing your false face feels 10x worse than running and hiding your real one. I think it's the desperate clawing to grab hold of something that's already out of reach. Trying to keep the seam together on something that's already torn to pieces. The bone-chilling inferiority that emerges from the sight of the real you. Raw and exposed.

You'll have to be alone, again. You'll have to risk it all, again. You'll have to be an antelope amongst hyenas, again. You'll have to be vulnerable, again. You'll have to be yourself.

You weren't ready, but God was. He grew tired of watching what he masterfully created pretend to be something else. So he shifted the atmosphere and caused the shape-shifting snakeskin to shed. The last seed you so coyishly protected slips from your grasp and lands headfirst in the pile of shit you've found yourself submerged in. Inevitably, growth is the only way out.

She was just a misunderstood girl from the eastside of Detroit with dreams of being anything other than poor and ordinary. She loved God, fiction books, love stories, and adventure. She lived through theatre, expressed through poetry, and rejoiced in dance. But she sang like her heart was on fire. She was art. Dying; yet destined to live again.

9. Oppression

I need freedom
From the oppression of my own mind
My past decisions terrorize my thoughts
Replaying like vivid horror movies

I remember when I used to get excited about marathons
Now, I'd give you everything I own if you could teach
me how to change this mental channel I'm stuck on

I thought time healed
But it only revealed
More trauma
More regret
I can't forget
I just keep analyzing
All the things I didn't see
All the things I'll never be
Oh how I wish I could just be free
Be happy
Be satisfied
With just being me

10. Regret

19

Anything the enemy gives stings longer than it satisfies.

11. Depression

Faceless, nameless criminal
you swiftly break and enter into the crevices of my mind
you steal my peace
and suddenly I'm left with dissatisfaction
For a faceless, nameless criminal you're beginning to feel
familiar
You're here everyday,
I mean you might as well introduce yourself
Who are you?
Depression

12. Villian

21

What happens when you find out you're the bad guy
living lies, camouflage and disguise
I've been fooling myself
but no one else
wondering why I can't make connection
discovering everyone see's the defects in my reflection
God my heart needs correction

13. Embracing Solitude

Embracing solitude
Learning to love the silence
It speaks volumes
God's Voice is Magnified in the Stillness

Who Am I ,
I question
You Are Mine
He Whispers

After I gave your flesh form
I blew intention into your body
Perfectly and Wonderfully Made
Made Specifically
Made to Love
Made to Praise
Made to Serve

I hid the best parts of you in Me
It is the glory of God to conceal a matter
To search out the matter is the glory of Kings.
There was Purpose in mind when I gave you life
Follow Me and You Find It

Let me unravel mysteries to you in the silence
What awaits in the unknown is
The Privilege of Purpose

Embracing Solitude.

14. I Know You Love Me

I know you love me
You paint the sky every night
illustrating stories with your paintbrush
You breathe life into the wind
Bring forth daises in the dessert
Everything you made is beautiful
You could not be anything less than love

Intricate architect
The way each planet is positioned perfectly
You made a galaxy for me to discover
You give me mysteries for me to wonder

Each element you petitioned
To take residency in this dimension
All to make the perfect world for me to live in
How could I ever consider you with apprehension
Oh I know you love me

15. Questioning My Father

Who Am I?
I Am That I Am

What Am I?
Beyond Human Comprehension

When Will I Show Myself?
You Experience Me Everyday

Where Am I?
Omnipresent

Where Have I Been?
I've been guardian to your life,
Watching over my friend.

Why Am I
Why Do You Ask Questions That You Will Never
Understand
Just Know That I Am, and Get to Know My Hand.

The Answers You Seek, Are Unraveled In My Plan
Follow My Son Closely
He'll Guide You into the Land

How Do You Know You Can Trust Me
Well How Many Times Can You Count
Without a Shadow of a Doubt
You Beat The Odds & Stayed Alive
When There's No Plausible Reason You Should've
Survived

The Questions You Ask
Aren't Really What You Want to Know
Let me Speak Now
It's time for you to Grow.

16. Galilee

Eternal water flows from you like Jordan
I'll follow the way of the current
I know you'll meet me wherever it leads

I'm content in the in-between
Because the victory is in the journey
Not the landmarks
Testimony is derived from what is endured inbetween
the highlights

Standing in between now and tomorrow
Your word matures in me
Your love grows
Understanding and wisdom takes hold
And I find peace
Standing still
Like Galilee

17. The Wait

I will wait

I will wait on you with joy

Your pace teaches me patience

I will wait on you with humility

Your correction gives me eyes to see

I will wait on you

Seeking you earnestly

Your words are alive

Sweet and sound serenity

They activate something within me

I will wait on you

Your moves are monumental

18.

Procrastination=Complacency

I wanna be something different
But I don't know how to change
Ashamed of my reflection
Tormented by another's perception
Because it only solidifies the thoughts I try to suppress
I clutch my chest
I can barely catch my breath between the tears
My worst fear
Growing up and becoming nothing
My life is series of dead ends and squandered
opportunities
I dreamed of changing tomorrow
But I can't even change myself
Every effort felt
Todays responsibilities become tomorrows trophy on the
shelf
I wanna be something different
I gotta do something different...
So, I guess I'll change tomorrow